IS MY SCHOOL
A BETTER SCHOOL
BECAUSE
I LEAD IT?

BARUTI K. KAFELE

IS MY SCHOOL A BETTER SCHOOL BECAUSE I LEAD IT?

ASCD

Alexandria, Virginia USA

1703 N. Beauregard St. • Alexandria, VA 22311-1714 USA
Phone: 800-933-2723 or 703-578-9600 • Fax: 703-575-5400
Website: www.ascd.org • E-mail: member@ascd.org
Author guidelines: www.ascd.org/write

Deborah S. Delisle, *Executive Director;* Stefani Roth, *Publisher;* Genny Ostertag, *Director, Content Acquisitions;* Julie Houtz, *Director, Book Editing & Production;* Joy Scott Ressler, *Editor;* Judi Connelly, *Associate Art Director;* Thomas Lytle, *Graphic Designer;* Keith Demmons, *Production Designer;* Mike Kalyan, *Director, Production Services;* Trinay Blake, *E-Publishing Specialist;* Audra Jefferson, *Production Specialist.*

All web links in this book are correct as of the publication date below but may have become inactive or otherwise modified since that time. If you notice a deactivated or changed link, please e-mail books@ascd.org with the words "Link Update" in the subject line. In your message, please specify the web link, the book title, and the page number on which the link appears.

PAPERBACK ISBN: 978-1-4166-2689-3   ASCD product #120013   n10/18
PDF E-BOOK ISBN: 978-1-4166-2691-6; see Books in Print for other formats.

Quantity discounts are available: e-mail programteam@ascd.org or call 800-933-2723, ext. 5773, or 703-575-5773. For desk copies, go to www.ascd.org/deskcopy.

Library of Congress Cataloging-in-Publication Data

Names: Kafele, Baruti K., author.
Title: Is my school a better school because I lead it? / Baruti K. Kafele.
Description: Alexandria, VA, USA : ASCD, [2018] | Includes bibliographical references and index.
Identifiers: LCCN 2018028037 (print) | LCCN 2018035494 (ebook) | ISBN 9781416626916 (PDF) | ISBN 9781416626893 (pbk.)
Subjects: LCSH: Educational leadership. | School management and organization.
Classification: LCC LB2805 (ebook) | LCC LB2805 .I17198 2018 (print) | DDC 371.2--dc23
LC record available at https://lccn.loc.gov/2018028037

27 26 25 24 23 22 21 20 19   1 2 3 4 5 6 7 8 9 10 11 12

This book is dedicated to my very first teachers and mentors of school leadership: Dr. Alease King, who was my principal when I was a 5th grade teacher and undergoing my administrative internship, and Dr. Kenneth King, my direct mentor, who became my "boss" when I became a principal in East Orange, New Jersey. Both of these great educators—who, I might add, are married to each other—gave me my initial leadership foundation, without which I wouldn't be the leader that I am today.

IS MY SCHOOL A BETTER SCHOOL BECAUSE I LEAD IT?

INTRODUCTION

I n 2015, my third book for ASCD, *The Principal 50: Critical Leadership Questions for Inspiring Schoolwide Excellence*, was published. Intended for current and aspiring school leaders, the book emphasizes "looking within" to inspire excellence in others; at its core are 50 self-reflective questions for educators to ponder that get to the heart of what it means to be an effective school leader.

I traveled around the United States and abroad to promote the book, engaging leaders in different parts of the world in discussions about the questions within it. In each of these discussions, I found myself returning to the same overarching question: "Is my school a better school *because* I lead it?" I would ask of school leaders, "Is your school a better school *because* you are there? Is there *something about you* that makes your school stand a better chance of success? Would your school be a better school if someone else were leading it instead of you?"

I was surprised by the reaction—or *lack* of reaction—school leaders had to my overarching question. Usually I was met with silence and had to prod for responses. This makes sense, as answering the question accurately requires us to be brutally honest with ourselves—even when the truth hurts—particularly in a public forum.

There are three key areas to consider when asking yourself if your school is better *because* you are there:

- Your contention,
- Your evidence, and
- Your staff's perception.

Your contention is easy—it's what you think, feel, and believe about your leadership. For your contention to be valid, *your evidence* must support it. If *your staff's perception* does not align to *your contention* or to *the evidence,* then a serious disconnect is present that needs to be addressed.

It is my strong belief that addressing and rectifying any disconnect between contentions and your evidence of leadership in schools begins with self-reflection and self-assessment, which can best be engaged in by asking and answering questions of ourselves.

We must be entirely frank and prepared to face truths that make us uncomfortable. I learned long ago that inspiration doesn't always last, but discomfort sticks around until the root issues are resolved. Though I have been called a "motivational speaker," I prefer to think of myself as a "discomfort speaker"—my objective is to create discomfort toward inspiring leadership excellence.

Before continuing with this book, I want you to briefly ponder the following question: "*Who* is that leading *my* school?" Have you ever stopped to consider *who you are as the leader of your school*, and how your leadership is being perceived by all parties? Have you ever *stepped outside of yourself* to scrutinize your own leadership with a critical eye? If so, what did you see? Did you like what you saw? Did you feel that what you were observing was the best possible version of yourself? Were you dissatisfied with what you saw? Did you see room for improvement? Did you see areas of concern that required your immediate attention?

The goal of this book is to help you examine your leadership identity and the value that it brings to your school. I sincerely hope that you do in fact feel some discomfort as you read the pages that follow and that you use that energy to rectify any underlying issues.

With all this said, let us now delve into the who, what, where, why, and when of your leadership approach. By the time you're finished with this book, I want you to be able to definitively say, "Yes! My school is a better school *because* I lead it!"

CHAPTER 1

My Leadership Identity—Who I Am

Q1: Who am I as the leader of my school?

Great leaders possess a very clear and evident leadership identity. Their leadership attributes are clearly visible, identifiable, and distinguishable. When you interact with them, you can sense their leadership. Consider, for example, one of the greatest leaders the world has ever known: Dr. Martin Luther King, Jr. There is no question who he was as a leader. We know who he was and what he represented by the way he conducted himself in his leadership capacity.

Clarity of identity leads to certain expectations. When I see a person in a pilot's uniform at the airport, for example, my expectation is not only that he or she will be flying a plane but also that the pilot has an expertise in flying planes. This is a result of my knowledge of his or her professional identity via the uniform. Your leadership identity in school should be as clearly distinguishable as a pilot's uniform, making a statement from the outset.

So, who *are* you as the leader of your school? Who are you once you put that "principal's uniform" on? What is it about your leadership that sets you apart from everyone else? The answers that you come up with are *your contention* of your identity as a leader—how you see yourself through your own set of lenses.

The ensuing challenge is to *identify evidence* that supports your contention of your leadership identity. Volume and quality of classroom visits and pre- and post-observation conferences are certainly data points to examine, for example, but the most important evidence is *your staff's perception* of your qualities as a leader. Do staff members feel that they have grown in their practice thanks to your instructional leadership? Is there in any way a disconnect between your contention and staff's perceptions of you?

Q2: Is who I think I am as the leader of my school consistent with the evidence?

It is easy to reflect upon who we are as school leaders and reach the wrong conclusion. I have engaged countless principals of challenging schools in conversations about the obstacles they face ensuring schoolwide success. Very often, they will attribute any problems to fellow staff, difficult parents, apathetic students, poverty, crime, drugs, and so on, without a word about their own leadership. In these educators' eyes, once all external factors are addressed, their leadership is bound to flourish.

This perspective ignores a central tenet of school leadership: effective leaders inspire excellence *regardless of factors outside their control*. If you believe you are a strong leader, you must earnestly examine the evidence at hand and ask yourself honestly: Does it support what I contend about myself? It is imperative that you see yourself objectively if you are to succeed as a leader in your school.

Q3: Is who I think I am as the leader of my school consistent with who my students and staff perceive me to be?

When you walk into your school every morning, are you the same person your students and staff perceive you to be? Every day, school leaders enter their buildings with a certain leadership identity. This may be a deliberate chosen presentation or one that you take for granted. In my case, I deliberately chose a leadership identity—though I had to adjust it during my early years of leadership.

In my first year as principal, I aspired to be like Joe Clark, the tough and unconventional but undoubtedly effective principal of an inner-city school portrayed in the 1989 movie *Lean on Me*. I figured that if I acted like Joe Clark, I would naturally achieve the same results.

I very quickly realized that this was a fantasy.

An effective leadership identity must be true to who you are as a leader, an educator, and a person while also modeling for staff and students how to carry oneself with dignity and professionalism. Just because principals don't work in the classroom doesn't mean they shouldn't teach! *Motivation and inspiration are methods of teaching.* Leadership itself is a series of lessons that you provide to students, staff, and even parents on how to approach matters big and small. Your leadership identity must exude enthusiasm for learning at every moment and with every individual; only then will others' perceptions of your abilities align with your own.

Once, before a presentation at a school in the Midwest, I met
with the principal in his office to discuss areas of concern
he might want me to address. During our discussion, the
principal boasted to me about his leadership abilities. Some
moments later, as he was introducing me to an auditorium
full of teachers, I realized how wrong this principal's contention was: the entire time he spoke, the audience kept talking
among themselves as though nobody was on stage. If this is
how they act here, I thought, imagine what the disconnect
reveals during regular school hours!

Q4: How does my leadership identity correlate with how I lead my school?

In leadership, the responsibilities are endless. As I always say
to my audiences, that one day where the principal can kick
back and say, "Yes, everything is done" just doesn't exist in the
world of a school leader. There is always work to be completed.
In fact, there is always urgent work to be completed—though
much of it your staff will never know about. A lot of leadership work is behind the scenes, unseen and therefore not
always factored into your identity by students and staff, but
taken into account by administrators at the district level. As
important as the work is that no one will ever see—budget-
ing, for example, or resource allocation—*teaching and learning*
must always be central to any leadership decisions in school.

School leaders wear countless hats to get the job done, and
those hats can change by the minute. For me personally, the
most important hat that I wore was that of "motivator." In fact,
it was the hat that mattered most to me relative to my students'
perception of me and my leadership. Students will never excel

if they are not inspired and eager to learn. Some kids come to school every day from unimaginably challenging home lives, and they especially must be motivated to grow in their education. That motivation starts with *you*, the school leader.

What about you? How does your leadership identity correlate with how you lead your school? What is it about your leadership identity that defines how you lead? Is your identity consistent from day to day? Does it drive you? Does it shape who you are, what you say, and how you act as a leader?

Q5: How do I mentally transition into my leadership identity every morning?

Throughout my years as a school leader, not a day went by that I didn't consider this question. I challenge you to do the same. In the mornings before you go to work, look at yourself in the mirror and make a brutally honest assessment of what you need to do to get into a frame of mind conducive to powerful leadership. You need to prepare to be at the top of your game every single day. Continuous self-reflection of this sort is essential for making the right adjustments to your leadership approach. Upon waking up in the morning, I would assess my attitude. I knew that I needed to have the right attitude if I was going to be productive on any given day. I used to continue the self-reflection in the car on my drive to work and yet again in front of my office mirror when I got to school. You can never be too mentally prepared to provide your school with the leadership it requires.

Do you have a mental preparation ritual? If so, what does it look like? If not, I highly encourage you to adopt one.

CHAPTER 2

My Leadership Presence—What I Represent

Q6: What does my leadership presence represent to my school?

There are so many different yet vital components to leadership that no single leader is ever going to master all of them. Our identities outside of school inform our leadership presence inside of it, affecting which aspects of leadership we focus on most. Those with self-confidence and a strong sense of mission will always be a step ahead in the leadership game.

When I worked as a substitute teacher early on in my career, I was in a different school or district every day, and one day has always stood out for me. I was at an urban high school in New Jersey that obviously "had it together" on every level. I could *feel* the principal's presence in the building—and I didn't even know who the principal was! About halfway through my visit, I finally saw him. The principal walked down the hall with an air of unmistakable authority. His presence telegraphed an utterly no-nonsense approach to education. It was immediately clear to me that he was a key factor in the school's success.

As a leader in your school, what does *your mere presence* in the building mean to the overall climate? What message does it convey? What does it represent? Does your presence alone play a role in meeting your intended objectives? What does your presence say without you ever opening your mouth? Is your leadership a positive, powerful, equitable, effective, hands-on, visionary presence in your school, even when you are not physically in the building? As I am known to say, when I walk through the school, I want to be able to "see the leadership" without "seeing the leadership."

Q7: What does my leadership presence represent to my students?

As a consultant, I get to see all sorts of schools throughout the United States and abroad. I see schools where students are excelling, schools where students are making steady progress, and schools where students are struggling. In my experience, the strength of a principal's leadership presence almost always has something to do with how well a school is performing.

When I served as a principal, I was always very much aware of what my presence meant to my students. There was nothing accidental about it; my presence was very much by design. Being in a predominantly black and urban setting, I knew that many of my students returned every day to home environments without any strong male role models. Both male and female students were bereft of the nurturing, guidance, leadership, and modeling that a father should ideally provide. It was part of my mission, then, to show them the difference between being a man and simply a male.

What does your leadership presence represent to your students? When they observe you, what exactly is it that they see? When they listen to you, what exactly is it that they hear? When they think of you, what connotations come to mind? Your leadership presence conveys a message to students whether you want it to or not; the question is whether you are in control of that message. You must get a firm handle on what your presence should mean to your students and convey that meaning with every word you speak and action you take.

Q8: What does my leadership presence represent to my staff?

In my workshops, I will often ask the administrators present if they are the instructional leaders of their schools. Principals will sometimes feel affronted by the question—"Of course I am! I'm the leader of the school, after all." When I ask them to reflect on *the evidence* for this assertion, these same principals will suddenly go silent. Self-reflection and consideration of the evidence is paramount here. Does staff perceive you as a leader who helps shape the direction of instruction in school?

As your staff is growing professionally, it is imperative that they can attribute at least some of their professional growth to their collegial relationship with you. If they see no evidence of your role in their development, then you have work to do proving otherwise.

Q9: What does my leadership presence represent to my students' parents?

It is a sad fact that far too many students are underperforming in schools all over the United States because their parents are simply not productively involved in their lives. When this is the case, it becomes incumbent upon the school to put mechanisms in place to increase parental engagement.

Recently, I held a workshop and served as a keynote speaker at a parent conference in Broward County, Florida. As I was driving to the conference center, the only thing on my mind was that I had this one opportunity to possibly affect the life of a child *through* his or her parents.

The room was packed for both sessions of my workshop, and parents were fully engaged, enthusiastically participating in call-and-response. My presence *mattered* in those two rooms. Those parents saw me as a source of valuable information, inspiration, and empowerment. I reminded the parents emphatically that, "You are the number one determinant of the success or failure of your children—you have power and influence over your children's outcomes." They yelled back at me, *Amen! YES! Say that!*

To cement a strong leadership presence among parents, maximize your visibility and interactions with parents during the school day and especially at school functions such as back-to-school nights. For students to receive the support they need to truly soar academically both at school and at home, it is crucial that educational leaders make themselves as available as possible to their families.

So, what does *your* leadership presence represent to your students' parents? Who you are in their eyes will greatly influence their degree of engagement in their children's educational lives.

Q10: What does my leadership presence represent to my school's community?

Educational leaders can ill-afford to isolate themselves or their schools from the neighborhoods that surround them, as they are inextricably entwined—yet it is all too common for them to become so absorbed in the day-to-day happenings of a school that they lose sight of the larger community. This was certainly the case for me in my early days in charge of leading a struggling school. I was focused so much on the bottom line of student achievement inside the building that I neglected to seek out and tap community resources to achieve this overarching goal.

Eventually, wisdom kicked in. Leveraging my speaking skills, I made myself available to present in any forum that would have me—religious institutions, community agencies, sports organizations, city hall, you name it. I wanted to tell our story—to share with the greater community what our students and teachers were accomplishing against all odds. I needed the people whose kids, grandkids, nephews, and nieces went to my school to know that we were giving them a world-class education.

Community engagement isn't a one-way street—I knew that there was much support and assistance available to draw upon. The area in which my school was located boasted a vibrant population from all walks of life who were eager to help our students excel. Over time, more and more community members came to be involved in such initiatives as our Young Men's and Young Women's Empowerment Program.

As referenced in my ASCD book *Motivating Black Males to Achieve in School and in Life* (2009), I brought men and women from the community into the school to assist us with the process of helping our students to navigate the challenges of life toward ultimately becoming upstanding young men and women beyond high school. This included mentorship, guidance, support, college visits, work visits, and the empowering messages that these community members consistently brought to our students.

What about you? Do you have a leadership presence in your school's community? Have you established your leadership beyond the walls of your school? Do members of the community recognize you when you're out and about?

CHAPTER 3

My Leadership Impact—My Influence

Q11: How does my leadership impact my school's brand identity?

The power of corporate branding is all around us. Many of us only purchase certain products and shop in certain stores because we are loyal to specific brands, most often due to their perceived superiority. Accrued perceptions likewise create a branding identity for your school. Your school's brand is its identity within the building and without. As a school community, you must be in control of your brand identity or the outside community will define it for you based on how they perceive it, which may be counterproductive and inconsistent with the brand you are trying to project.

Your school's brand will be as attractive as your leadership is strong, clear, and effective. If you strive for excellence at all times while ensuring a supportive environment for all, both your leadership identity and your school's brand will be the envy of others. It is incumbent upon you to discuss with staff regularly how you wish for your school to be seen by the community and, most important, *to work consciously and consistently at achieving this end.*

Does your school's brand inspire loyalty? How does your leadership impact your school's brand? Does your school's brand accurately reflect the climate, culture, and performance at your school? Does your staff understand the significance of your school's brand? Have you and your staff helped to mold the brand, or has it evolved haphazardly without your influence? Does your school's brand matter to *you*?

Q12: How does my leadership impact my school's *mission* and *vision*?

Put simply, a school's mission refers to *what the school is about*, and its vision to *where the school is going.* Your school's mission is the foundation upon which it stands. A school that is serious about its mission ensures that the mission statement is known to all—perhaps even recited by students and staff every morning. The same is true of a school's vision statement. As the leader of the school, you must see to it that both mission and vision statements are posted throughout the building, including in all classrooms.

True leadership means ensuring that the school is "walking" in its mission and vision daily. Everything in the school should be scrutinized through the dual lens of mission and vision, including (and most especially) student achievement scores. Mission and vision statements should be seen as living documents that drive the work of the school.

How does your leadership impact your school's mission and vision? Do you prioritize internalization of values related to the mission and vision? Are your school's mission and vision known to the community at large? Do they drive the work in your building? Do students and staff "walk" in your mission and vision? Is your mission and vision recited by your school community daily?

Q13: How does my leadership impact my school's climate and culture?

When I worked as a principal, I had a quiet ritual that I would engage in every year. On the nights before, of, and following graduation, I would enter the school's empty auditorium, sit where the graduates sat, and reflect deeply on the previous year as well as on the one to come.

On the first two nights, foremost on my mind was whether we had provided our graduates with an adequate overall environment for learning that would allow them to succeed in the future. On the third night, I would turn my thoughts to the incoming students, pondering whether our school's climate and culture were sufficiently welcoming while considering what adjustments would need to be made going into the start of the next school year. Starting with that third night, I was obsessed with what students would see, hear, feel, and experience throughout their first day of the new school year and beyond. This ritual was important to me, helping bring closure to the current school year while also building a bridge to the next one.

A school's climate can be likened to a collective mood and its culture to a shared lifestyle. In both cases, modeling begins at the top. Creating a climate and a culture that inspires and motivates students needs to be a priority. Another strategy I employed as a principal was twofold: a daily morning message, coupled with ongoing monthly meetings with students in small groups divided by grade and gender. I used these meetings to discuss anything and everything, but always with a view toward developing the climate and culture in a positive direction.

What do your students *see, hear, feel,* and *experience* as they walk into your building every morning, and how do they *act* when they're there? How do their actions affect the school's mood? What do you, as the school's leader, do to ensure that the mood is positive, vibrant, and focused on academic excellence?

Q14: How does my leadership impact the social-emotional needs of my students?

I have always chosen to work in urban schools with students of color from high-poverty environments, as I feel these schools can benefit the most from my specific skillset while also offering me the most professional fulfillment. Too often, the home experiences of students from these kinds of schools are unimaginable to educators and staff. This disconnect has profound implications for school leadership, because these same children walk through your front doors every day bringing their pain along with them.

Whenever I visit a school, I look for evidence that the principal is focused on meeting students' social-emotional needs. This can be something as simple as greeting students, preferably by name, as they arrive on campus, or delivering an uplifting and empowering message over the PA every morning.

Are the social-emotional needs of your students being met in your school? Are they a priority under your leadership? Are structures in place to ensure students' emotional safety and security? What programs are in place for your students to help meet students' needs? Two programs that I have really liked over the years are peer counseling and restorative practices that enable students to be deeply engaged with one another in a variety of different situations.

Q15: How does my leadership impact my school's academic performance?

As a football fan, it's always interesting to observe the excitement around the Super Bowl every year. It reminds me of classroom visits of some school administrators, actually. Let me explain.

The football season for the most part attracts true football fans—people who both know and enjoy the game. They know the "Xs and the Os" of football. In other words, they know plays, they know offenses, and they know defenses. When a play goes awry, they understand why. When a play works, they also understand why. They know the players and their positions. They know the coaches and their assignments. They know penalties, and they know a bad call by a referee when they see one. In other words, they know football and they know the game inside and out.

The Super Bowl, on the other hand, in addition to attracting hard-core football fans, attracts casual fans and nonfans—those who don't really follow football and know little to nothing about the details of the game. But because it is Super Bowl time, which brings with it media intrigue and hype, many nonfans watch the game. Because they aren't "true" fans of the game, they don't really know what they are watching. They just want to see the execution of a good play—or maybe a good hit, a nice pass, or a long run for a score. Therefore, they are easily dazzled and impressed in a way that the "true" fan would not be.

You might be asking, "What's this got to do with leadership impact on academic performance?" Everything! Just as there are these two types of fans, there are also two types of school leaders who visit classrooms to observe instruction.

One type of leader thoroughly understands good pedagogy. This leader goes into the classroom with his or her own philosophy, beliefs, opinions, and ideas about how children learn and how they correlate with the instruction being observed. This leader understands that children learn differently and is therefore looking closely to see how the teacher's instructional strategies are benefiting all of the learners as opposed to only a few. In other words, this leader is checking that the teacher is implementing equitable strategies that ensure that all of the students have an opportunity to learn.

The other type of leader, on the other hand, lacks a philosophy, beliefs, opinions, and ideas about how children learn. Like the nonfan referenced above, this leader is therefore easily dazzled and impressed by what appears to look like good instruction. In other words, although the teaching being observed "looks good," this leader isn't bringing a frame of reference of what works best for all of the learners in the classroom. Instead, via the motions and actions of the teacher, he or she has resolved that the instruction being observed is good instruction for all. This leader's leadership, therefore, adversely impacts the school's academic performance (because his or her actions are comparable to that of the nonfan—who doesn't really understand the game).

School leaders must be prepared to engage as instructional leaders who fully understand instruction and work toward ultimately impacting the academic performance of their schools.

CHAPTER 4

My Leadership Mission—My What

Q16: What's that one thing over all of my responsibilities that I deem I simply must accomplish?

Your *mission* and your *work* are two totally separate entities. The latter includes a lot of drudgery—endless paperwork, interminable meetings, all manner of administrative duties— that may or may not align to the former. It is crucial to identify the work responsibilities that are most vital to your leadership mission if you are to succeed in improving your school. Whereas work deadlines can keep you up at night with worry, your mission should fill you with hope and inspire you to always work toward achieving student excellence.

Choosing your mission and figuring out the duties that are essential to fulfilling it are very personal decisions that should be based on what aspects of leadership move you the most. In my case, having grown up as the black son of a single mother and therefore being all too aware of the attendant challenges, *empowering male students of color* became my mission without a second thought. To this end, when I became a principal, I made sure that my work responsibilities included developing and piloting a Young Men's Empowerment Program. As far as I'm aware, this was the first program of its sort in the country. We dressed our young men up in shirts, ties, slacks, shoes, and a belt and brought in male speakers and mentors to provide inspiration and leadership. This program consumed my thinking;

I wasn't going to rest easy until I saw the results I sought to achieve. It was personal—and it suited my mission perfectly.

What work do you do that is tied specifically to your personal leadership mission? What are you most passionate about? What work duties excite you and inspire you to continue in your journey as a leader?

Q17: What fuels my passion for leadership every day?

At some point before you became a principal, you surely came to the realization that *you wanted to lead*. Your passion was driven by something. What was it then, and what is it now, specific to your leadership, that raises your students' chances of success? Like a vehicle, passion needs fuel if it is to be sustained. Are you concerned that students won't apply themselves in school without the direction you can afford them? Are you eager to make your school an oasis of peace, calm, and focus for students with violent or chaotic home lives? Identify and examine the primary catalyst for pursuing your leadership journey.

Q18: Do my leadership actions reflect my leadership mission?

No doubt you have met school leaders who can talk all day long about how great they are but whose *leadership actions* do not back up their words. *How you act* as a leader must align to your leadership mission—*what you are about*. You cannot claim to be a strong instructional leader, for example, if you never visit classrooms, or that you are strong on discipline if the climate of your school is toxic. You cannot say you are a strong relationship-builder if just the thought of you turns everyone off. You cannot say that you are all about your students if you don't even know their names. And you cannot demand that others remain calm in challenging situations if you appear worked up whenever the pressure is on.

Q19: What is the evidence that I am walking in my leadership mission where school safety is concerned?

The pressure on school leaders to keep our students safe has risen exponentially in recent years due to a proliferation of widely publicized mass shootings. As a new administrator entering the field in 1998—one year before the massacre at Columbine that precipitated our current epidemic—the thought of a gunman showing up in the building was among the furthest things from educators' minds. In the intervening years, it has rapidly become a three-alarm priority.

We can never truly guarantee that no student will be harmed if an intruder with intent to kill accosts the school, but part of your leadership mission *must* include a solemn oath that you *will do everything in your power* to keep every student safe in the event of a life-threatening crisis. Take preemptive action: for example, every school principal should develop, distribute, and discuss a crisis-management plan that addresses as many contingencies as possible. Does every staff member know his or her role in every emergency situation? Is everyone conversant in the finer points of the plan? What about students? Do they know *their* roles in different scenarios? How often does your school hold emergency drills to prepare for the event of an intruder?

Are the drills carried out to perfection? What is the school's relationship to the local police department and hospitals?

I am certain that I annoyed a lot students and staff with the many lockdown drills I conducted in my years as an administrator, but achieving perfection is necessary. This is what drills are for, after all.

Q20: How does my leadership mission impact the overall academic performance of my school?

The bottom line of your leadership lies in your students' academic performance. As I previously noted, my leadership mission had at its core the empowerment of my boys. I trust I don't have to go into detail here as to why I felt young men of color, especially those from black and Latino families, required the full measure of my support. But empowerment alone is useless without tangible results, so I made sure that it led to a concomitant rise in student achievement.

Does your leadership mission correlate with the academic performance of your students? Have you defined your *academic* mission? Does it drive your academic focus daily? Is your staff in sync with your leadership *mission* for your school? Your answers to these questions are crucial to the overall academic performance of your students.

CHAPTER 5

My Leadership Purpose—My Why

Q21: What is my leadership purpose?

Your leadership *purpose* and leadership *mission* are related, but separate. If the latter represents the "what" of leadership, the former represents the "why." Your leadership mission is only as significant as the purpose driving it. Leadership purpose is the engine that will sustain your mission over the long haul.

As I mentioned in Chapter 4, my mission has always been to empower young men of color, particularly those from challenging life environments. But *why* was this my mission? What *purpose* did I have for pursuing this overarching goal no matter the obstacles? The empowerment of these young men was my mission *because* the data clearly showed that without it, their chances of advancement in life would be perilously slim. My *purpose,* therefore, was to provide enough motivation and direction for these young men to establish a pattern of behaviors that would guarantee a future of boundless success.

What is the engine that drives your leadership mission? What are you striving for above all else in your leadership work? Deep down, what makes you *need* to be leader?

Q22: What is the evidence that I am walking in my leadership purpose?

We all join the ranks of school leaders with the best of intentions, but do the results indicate that our work is truly making a difference in students' lives? What is your "daily walk"? What is your evidence?

Evidence is a strong word. It says to a person, "prove it!" As indicated in the Introduction, in addition to having your contention, you must also have the *evidence* to support your contention. For example, one can state that they are doing all they can to achieve a particular goal and conclude that the goal is unreachable. My first question to this individual would be, "What is the evidence that you have done all that you can? Delineate for me everything that you have done to achieve the goal." As the person lists all of the activities, it will turn out that there are a many activities that haven't been explored. Therefore, the evidence that the individual has exhausted all options toward reaching the goal is simply not there.

I often look at the "leadership why" through both a micro lens and a macro lens. Here, I want to look at the "why" through a micro lens followed by an explanation through the macro lens.

Why do you report to your school as the principal or one of the leaders every day? Why do you get up early in the morning? Why do you put in the enormous number of hours and work daily? Why do you every day endure the inordinate pressures, demands, challenges, and obstacles that accompany school leadership? This is not easy work you have chosen. It ranks amongst some of the most challenging and stressful work that one could engage in…but you do it anyway. In other words, why do you do this work? What is your "why"?

My mission with regard to the Young Men's Empowerment Program was to build men out of boys and my "why" was because of all of the alarming statistics about the young men in my demographic throughout the United States That was very specific and very personal. That was through my micro lens of my leadership "why." Looking at my leadership through my macro lens, I walked into that school every morning because I simply wanted to inspire my students, in an urban school comprising predominantly economically disadvantaged at-risk children of color, to believe in themselves and their possibilities. That is, I took on a school leadership role so that I could put myself in position to "motivate, educate, and empower" an entire student population rooted in a reality where so many of this demographic fail to live up to their potential. This was my "why" through my macro lens.

Your contention is the easy part, however. In fact, your contention is typically quite noble. I think that practically everyone who enters school leadership enters with the best of intentions, but what's key is your evidence. Does your evidence support your intention and your contention? I converse with countless school leaders across the United States They share with me what they are currently doing and what they intend to accomplish. I listen attentively. But what I really want to see is the evidence of the contention. Not only do I want to see the results—I want to see the "walk." I want to see the evidence of everything they contend to be and to accomplish. I keep using the example of instructional leadership due to its significance toward the success of a school, so when I hear a school leader talk about the role he plays toward the academic success of his school, my focus is on the evidence and, in this case, on whether or not this leader is in fact an instructional leader. Therefore, I am looking for evidence of all of the components of effective instructional leadership.

As the leader of your school, it is imperative then that your reason for assuming school leadership—your "why"—is supported with evidence, which is your daily walk. When your "walk" mirrors your "talk," the probability for school leadership success is very high.

Q23: How does my leadership purpose impact student and staff performance?

Whenever I visit a school, some of the signs of purpose in action that I look for are those embedded in interactions among school leaders, students, and staff.

I recall one school visit during which the assistant principal showed me around the building. He was nervous and unsure of himself and seemed awkward when we entered classrooms— most likely because he was only accustomed to going in for the purpose of disciplining students rather than routinely to ensure student needs were being met. I felt bad for this fellow, who I knew would never make an effective school leader as long as his responsibilities were confined to addressing student discipline. And yet, when I asked him what made him want to be a school leader, he told me his goal was to give children hope. I asked him if he felt that he was walking in his purpose, and he openly admitted that he wasn't. He said that he'd been relegated by the culture of the school to being a full-time disciplinarian and thus had lost his "why." I asked him if he and his principal had discussed his role beyond being the appointed disciplinarian, and he said no. He said that he felt trapped in this role, and there was little to nothing he could do about it. This saddened me not only for him but for the children and the teachers he supervised. How could this "leader" accurately evaluate teachers if his leadership practices have nothing to do with advancing their professional development?

Q24: What is the relationship between my leadership purpose and opportunities for student success?

Recently, I spoke to young men at an alternative high school for "last chance" students with criminal histories. As the young men entered the room to hear me speak, I could see the innocence in their eyes despite their troubled realities. I thought to myself, if only they knew how brilliant they are. If only they knew how *extraordinary* they are. If only they knew that the sky was truly their limit if only they'd make some simple adjustments in their lives. Easier said than done, but definitely doable.

Earlier that same day, I had presented at another high school to an entirely different audience: student leaders preparing for college. As I drove back to the airport that evening I thought to myself, did the purpose of the leaders at the two schools provide the young men among their ranks with equitable opportunities for success? If the needs of the at-risk students had been met when they were at their sending schools, could they have been saved from attending the alternative school? Were all options exhausted before the decision was made to transfer the young men? Did they have access to the programs and services that they needed to cope in the regular environment?

Many school leaders wouldn't last 10 minutes in some of their students' shoes, yet these are great kids—*brilliant* kids. Unfortunately, they must survive under such difficult conditions that their social-emotional needs have grown far greater than those of their peers. As the leader of your school, how do you ensure that the needs of your most challenged students are being met *where they are*? How do you ensure that they have the same opportunities for success as classmates with fewer obstacles before them? What is the relationship between your leadership purpose and your students' opportunities for success? Do you hold high expectations—including college enrollment—for *all* your students, including those with few role models in that respect? I would encourage you to expose such kids as much as possible to college graduates, current college students, college campuses, and college professors and administrators so that they can envision a concrete future.

Q25: How does my leadership purpose drive my overall leadership and decision making?

Reflect on when you initially thought that you wanted to lead a school. You probably thought to yourself that, if given the opportunity, no hurdle would be too high for you to surmount in the service of student excellence. There was a very specific reason that you wanted to lead and, as we have discussed, very specific goals that you wanted to accomplish. Your purpose was well defined—you knew exactly what you wanted to achieve. Does that sound about right? I know it describes me perfectly. I thought, "Once I'm in that leadership seat, my students will immediately soar to new heights." Turns out it wasn't that easy, though.

Leadership can certainly be tough going at first, but for the sake of your students, you must make the effort. The harder you work, and the more your work is driven by a passionate purpose, the more successful your journey becomes.

Never allow your leadership purpose to be compromised. When you are at your most overwhelmed by minutiae, when you are drowning in paperwork, when you have more decisions to make *now* than there is time in the day—*always keep your purpose to the forefront.* As long as you spend all your brainpower reacting to a barrage of stimuli, there is no way you are going to be able to take the reins and lead your school to true greatness. Your original purpose will be rendered irrelevant by the reality you've chosen. It is crucial, then, that you continually examine the dynamics in your school for any that may be veering you away from what you became a leader to do and why.

CHAPTER 6

My Leadership Vision—My Where

Q26: What is my leadership vision?

When I first began my leadership journey as the principal of
Sojourner Truth Middle School in East Orange, New Jersey, I
had the audacity to approach my superintendent and ask him
if I could develop a schoolwide pedagogical program responsive to all learners. The racial composition of the student body
was about 98 percent Black and 2 percent Latino. I wanted to
develop a program that capitalized on this reality. Specifically,
as a magnet middle school, we were the School of Science
and Technology. I proposed to the superintendent that we
add African-Centered Studies as a theme to our existing
theme and that we incorporate African and African American history electives to support the new theme. Additionally,
I wanted the overall theme of the school to be African-centered, which would include guest speakers/lecturers, programs,
assemblies, activities, and field trips—again to reflect the racial
composition of the student body while enabling us to be truly
culturally responsive to our student body (which necessitated
the inclusion of an examination of our current curriculum to
ensure that it, too, was culturally responsive to our student
population). The superintendent approved, but only on con-
dition that I show evidence of the program's efficacy. I asked
him to give me three years—the time it would take for my
incoming 6th graders to become 8th graders—and I would
make sure our school was number one in the district. Not only

did this happen at the middle school level, but we also became number one in the entire State of New Jersey among disadvantaged, predominantly African American middle schools. I had a leadership vision and followed it through, so I was able to claim no small degree of ownership over our results. I could *see* what we could accomplish at Sojourner Truth; all we had to do was get there.

What is *your* leadership vision for your school—not the school's or district's, but yours personally? What do you foresee that your school will accomplish *because* you are the leader? Are you *locked into* your leadership vision? Are staff and students aligned to your leadership vision?

Your school cannot afford for you to be the same person next year on this date that you are today. You have got to be able to demonstrate growth. To this end, you must attend leadership conferences and institutes and interact with other leaders. In no way can you afford to be stagnant, to assume that your current level of effectiveness will carry over into subsequent years. You must also be able to continuously adapt your leadership approach to changes in society and the world.

Q27: What is the evidence I am walking in my leadership vision?

What is it that you say over the course of a day that confirms that you are walking in your leadership vision? Early on in my leadership journey, I had a strong vision but no evidence whatsoever that I was truly walking in it. Most of my time was spent bogged down with discipline issues. It was only when I learned more about the overriding importance of positive culture and climate that I was able to readjust my approach to better align with my vision.

What is your leadership vision? What is the evidence that you are walking in it? Do you notice when you are deviating from the path laid out by your vision? If so, do you readjust your approach? How?

Q28: How do I get my staff to buy into my leadership vision?

If you are new to a school that has had a long history of stagnation or worse, you may need to persuade staff to buy into your vision. Teachers may feel worn down and burnt out based on the climate, culture, and conditions you inherited and the leadership that you replaced. You have much to correct. What will you do? Where will you start? How will you make sure your vision is followed?

You must begin by communicating your vision to everyone. A school that desperately needs leadership is usually one accustomed to new leaders arriving with big objectives, failing to meet them, and leaving. Staff members are disillusioned and skeptical that you can really make any difference. In their eyes, you will be gone soon, too. Attitudes can change—but only if you communicate and walk in your vision daily.

You must lead in every respect—and that includes listening. In staff meetings, during PLCs, and even one on one, you must provide your staff with as many opportunities as possible to add their input to your vision for the school. They must know that they have your attention in all matters related to student progress. Do not impose your vision—you want staff to buy into it and hold collective ownership of it. You must therefore build solid relationships by building trust. Staff must know that you are committed to being at your school over the long haul, so it is "safe" to buy into your vision. And once this occurs—once everyone is on board the leadership vision you have brought to the school with you—your leadership vision and the school's vision will have become one.

Q29: What are my leadership goals and plans toward fulfilling my leadership vision?

At the end of the day, having a personal vision of a destination is the easy part—the real challenge is in building the staircase that gets you there. *Short-term goals* for fulfilling your vision constitute the steps in this staircase. To make sure you're continuously climbing, be sure to write out each goal and assign a deadline to it.

As the saying goes, "a goal without a plan is just a wish"—and a wish is just not enough for effective school leadership. As important as your goals are, you must also have a strategy in place toward meeting them or you are just leading on impulse. A blueprint is essential. Once you have written out both your short-term goals and the plan which they compose, be sure to review them regularly. You want to keep both of them at the forefront of your thinking. To that end, what are your short- and long-term leadership goals? Are short- and long-term goals important to your leadership practice? Have you written a plan of action to accompany your leadership goals? How often do you review your goals and plan, and are they visible or easily accessible to review? Are your leadership goals and plan an indispensable component of your overall leadership?

Q30: What is my vision for my own professional growth and development?

When I was a new principal, I knew that professional development was important, but I was so overwhelmed by my duties that I treated it as a chore to be avoided. I had to grow into an understanding that my own growth was vital if I was to sustain my effectiveness.

Leaders are readers, and they learn from other leaders. Effective school leaders read regularly despite—or more precisely, to help guide—the long hours that they invest every day toward ensuring student excellence. They have such an *obsession with growing as leaders* that they carve out the necessary time. They have a vision of where they *will* be professionally, and they pore over roadmaps that can get them there. They understand that school leadership is not a nine-to-five—there is work to be done before and after school in the area of professional development. Strong leaders interact with other leaders as often as they can, particularly with successful veterans who have already solved the issues with which they may be grappling.

What books, journals, or articles are you reading to inform your leadership? What conferences, workshops, institutes, or seminars are you or will you be attending to improve your practice? As the leader of your school, what do you envision learning that you don't currently know? What goals do you have to fulfill this vision? Where do you see yourself one year from now regarding your professional growth? Two years from now? Five years from now?

CHAPTER 7

My Leadership Value—My Worth

Q31: Are my students better *because* I lead them?

When I asked this question at a recent leadership workshop, there was a long silence before a principal stood up to answer.

> My students are achieving at high levels, but it's not because of me—it's thanks to my dedicated staff, who are energetic, enthusiastic, and collaborative and they love their work. They are a family.

I listened to his words closely then responded.

> I appreciate everything you just said, but allow me to give you another perspective, Imagine if we took your staff and airlifted them to another school, but in this case with a leader who doesn't stress camaraderie, or who makes coming to work an uncomfortable chore for staff. Do you think they would exhibit anywhere near the same levels of energy, enthusiasm, and collaboration? These characteristics are in large part a function of *your* leadership.

Is there a *direct correlation* between your leadership of the school and student outcomes? Can you confidently say that your leadership is a catalyst for staff contentment and student progress? When all is said and done, you must be able to embrace the fact that whether your students succeed or fail is deeply rooted in your own leadership.

Q32: Are my teachers better *because* I lead them?

Many years ago, an administrative internship mentor said to me: "The purpose of your supervision of teachers will be the continued improvement of instruction." These words have stayed with me all this time; indeed, I regularly used the phrase as a barometer of my effectiveness. I have no problem admitting that I came up short on many occasions as I was learning the ins and outs of school leadership.

Are your teachers effective because you lead them? Are they *less* effective because you lead them? Can you identify what it is specifically about your leadership that either motivates or drags down your staff? What role do you play in helping to make your teachers effective? Are you able to gauge your teachers' professional growth accurately every year as a result of the work that you do with them? Besides your collegial relationship with your teachers, with what professional development resources do you provide them? When you walk into classrooms, is your role in what's happening evident?

Q33: Is parent engagement better *because* I lead the effort?

It's become a motto for me: *That which is a priority is that which gets done.* And yet, too often, we don't make the essential component of parent engagement a priority in our schools.

Teachers know all about the correlation between a lack of parental engagement and undesirable student outcomes (both academic and behavioral).

What are you, as the leader of your school, doing to address their concerns? Is parental engagement a priority of your leadership? If not, why not? If so, what is the evidence?

Deep, ongoing parental engagement means a lot more than enduring the occasional gripe session. Leadership must focus on strategies to work with parents toward their children's success both at school and in the home.

Q34: Are community relations better *because* I lead the effort?

Consider the following two hypothetical schools:

School A is a struggling school in a rural area. Relations between students and staff are hostile; both the climate and culture are toxic. Staff members do not enjoy working in the school, and turnover rate is alarmingly high. Students habitually underperform and exhibit undesirable behaviors. As soon as you walk into the hallway or any given classroom, you know immediately that you are in an environment that requires immediate attention. Parents complain about the school regularly to anyone willing to listen. Most only show up at the school to either complain about it or to return their children from suspension. The school's reputation in the community is atrocious. You are hard-pressed to find anyone who has anything nice to say about School A.

School B was the mirror image of School A just four short years ago—until the superintendent stepped in and replaced the principal. A purpose-driven, mission-oriented, visionary leader was brought into the school, and one of his very first initiatives was to reach out to all community stakeholders. He knew that if he could utilize the services of this diverse body of human capital, the implications for the school would be enormous. He immediately began reaching out to local agencies, governmental officials, business owners, and others in the community. Not only did he visit them, but he also invited them to the school for a communitywide forum to discuss his vision for the school and what roles they could all play toward making it become reality, including through mentorship programs. Over a very short time, School B became a high-performing school. Why? Because of a *change in leadership*.

As the leader of your school, do you have a productive relationship with the surrounding community? What role does the community play toward the success of your school? Are community partnerships a priority of your leadership?

Q35: Is my school a better school *because* I lead it?

During my time as a principal, I asked myself this question daily because it mattered so much to me. In my mind I always thought, "Why do they need me if the school isn't better *because* of me?" This was my daily fuel. My focus was always student achievement, but I was keenly aware that there was a direct correlation between my leadership effectiveness and student outcomes. I therefore held myself personally accountable for the success of my school.

Many of you reading this book are either aspiring school leaders or assistant principals who aspire to become principals. I want to remind you all that landing a job as a principal is simply not good enough. That's only the first step. Now you have to lead. Once you have acquired your position, any honeymoon period will be brief. You have to prove that you belong quickly. Results matter. The school *must* become a better school because *you* are there. It may not soar to the top of the ranks overnight, but progress must be evident and continual.

Challenge yourself daily. Find time in your daily schedule to just engage in the process of self-reflection and self-assessment. Ask yourself that most important question: "Is my school a better school because I lead it?" Be brutally honest with yourself and examine all the indicators. Although you are not leading alone or in a vacuum, everything that happens in your school is reflective of your leadership. Always remain cognizant of that reality.

FINAL THOUGHTS

Will your current diet and exercise regimen allow you to sustain your leadership over the long haul?

You probably weren't expecting this question, but it's important. When I was a classroom teacher, I quickly developed a fast-food diet because I was so busy I felt I didn't have enough time for much more. Things only got worse when I became an administrator and staff would bring me lunch. To make matters worse, I barely exercised—sure, I'd walk up and down the halls and stairwells, but I had no structured fitness routine.

When I became a full-time education consultant and speaker in 2011, at first my diet and sedentary habits became even more dire thanks to constant travel. My weight was increasing rapidly, my clothes were getting tighter, but I was oblivious to the warning signs. In my mind, health crises happened only to "other people."

On May 1, 2015, at the age of 54, in the middle of a 60-minute keynote address at the University of Miami, I had a heart attack—right on the stage.

The pain was intense, but through sheer determination and ignorance of what I was experiencing—left-side pain, dizziness, profuse sweating, unquenchable thirst—I finished my speech before being rushed to the hospital for life-saving surgery. My left main coronary artery—the main artery of the heart—was 100 percent clogged with plaque buildup, leading to a particularly severe kind of heart attack known colloquially as "the widow-maker."

And then I found out I had diabetes!

So, what's my point here? What does any of this have to do with leadership? It's very simple: I don't want you to make the mistake that I made. Don't assume that your body is a machine that can endure anything. It is not, and it cannot. It has to be treated correctly. I now walk and run on a treadmill daily and eat a healthy diet. I take care of myself. Yes, it adds more time to my schedule and yes, the food is more expensive, but I can now live to continue spreading my message.

I want the same for you—*without* the heart attack. Your school, your staff—and most important of all, your students—need you to be healthy and vigorous to lead them.

Finally, this is the ninth book I have written since 1990. I can honestly say that I enjoyed writing it more than the previous eight because of its theme and content. As with all my books, it is a quick read laced with self-reflective questions, but it is also an ongoing study and reference book. I encourage you to keep this book close by as you continue to navigate the challenges of school leadership.

This book is about *you*. It is about your leadership identity, presence, impact, mission, purpose, vision, and value to your school. My hope is that reflecting on the questions and ideas in these pages will lead to rich discussions and leadership planning for you and your staff.

So once again, ask yourself: Is my school a better school *because* I lead it?

BIBLIOGRAPHY

Hosey, A. (2017). *Superhero status: A superhero guide to leadership.* Powder Springs, GA: Garnett Publishing.

Kafele, B. (2013). *Closing the attitude gap: How to fire up your students to strive for success.* Alexandria, VA: ASCD.

Kafele, B. (2015). *The principal 50: Critical leadership questions for inspiring schoolwide excellence.* Alexandria, VA: ASCD.

Kafele, B. (2016). *The teacher 50: Critical questions for inspiring classroom excellence.* Alexandria, VA: ASCD.

Linton, C. (2011). *The equity framework.* Thousand Oaks, CA: Corwin.

Lopez, N. (2016). *The bridge to brilliance.* New York: Viking.

Muhammad, A. (2009). *Transforming school culture: How to overcome staff division.* Bloomington, IN: Solution Tree.

Parrett, W. H. & Budge, K. M. (2012). *Turning high-poverty schools into high-performing schools.* Alexandria, VA: ASCD.

Schwanke, J. (2016). *You're the principal! Now what?: Strategies and solutions for new school leaders.* Alexandria, VA: ASCD.

Sterrett, W. (2011). *Insights into action: Successful school leaders share what works.* Alexandria, VA: ASCD.

INDEX

ABOUT THE AUTHOR

 **Baruti K. Kafele**, a highly regarded urban educator in New Jersey for more than 20 years, is a distinguished master teacher and transformational school leader. As an elementary school teacher in East Orange, NJ, he was named East Orange School District and Essex County Public Schools Teacher of the Year, and he was a finalist for New Jersey State Teacher of the Year. As a middle and high school principal, he led the transformation of four different New Jersey urban schools, including Newark Tech—transforming it from a low-performing school in need of improvement to national recognition—recognized by *U.S. News and World Report* as one of America's best high schools.

Kafele, one of the most sought-after education speakers in North America, is the author of eight books, including his four ASCD best sellers—*Closing the Attitude Gap, Motivating Black Males to Achieve in School and in Life, The Principal 50,* and *The Teacher 50.* He is the recipient of more than 150 educational, professional, and community awards, including the prestigious Milken National Educator Award and the National Alliance of Black School Educators Hall of Fame Award. As well, he was inducted into the East Orange, New Jersey Hall of Fame, and the City of Dickinson, Texas, proclaimed February 8, 1998 Baruti Kafele Day. Kafele can be reached via his website—www.principalkafele.com.

Related ASCD Resources

At the time of publication, the following resources were available (ASCD stock numbers appear in parentheses):

Print Products

The Teacher 50: Critical Leadership Questions for Inspiring Classroom Excellence by Baruti K. Kafele (#117009)

The Principal 50: Critical Leadership Questions for Inspiring Schoolwide Excellence by Baruti K. Kafele (#115050)

Closing the Attitude Gap: How to Fire Up Your Students to Strive for Success by Baruti K. Kafele (#114006)

Motivating Black Males to Achieve in School and in Life by Baruti K. Kafele (#109013)

Align the Design: A Blueprint for School Improvement by Nancy Mooney and Ann Mausbach (#108005)

Results Now: How We Can Achieve Unprecedented Improvements in Teaching and Learning by Mike Schmoker (#106045)

Schooling by Design: Mission, Action, and Achievement by Grant Wiggins and Jay McTighe (#107018)

What Works in Schools: Translating Research into Action by Robert J. Marzano (#102271)

Digital Products

DVD: *Motivating Black Males to Achieve in School and in Life* by Baruti K. Kafele (#611087)

For up-to-date information about ASCD resources, go to www.ascd. org. You can search the complete archives of *Educational Leadership* at www.ascd.org/el.

ASCD myTeachSource®

Download resources from a professional learning platform with hundreds of research-based best practices and tools for your classroom at http://myteachsource.ascd.org/.

For more information, send an e-mail to member@ascd.org; call 1-800-933-2723 or 703-578-9600; send a fax to 703-575-5400; or write to Information Services, ASCD, 1703 N. Beauregard St., Alexandria, VA 22311-1714 USA.